THE WORLD WIDE WEB

Is and How to Use It

http://wwww

3 4028 08910 3320
HARRIS COUNTY PUBLIC LIBRARY

D1003329

WITHDRAWN

J 025.042 Yea
Yearling, Tricia,
The World Wide Web : what it is
and how to use it /
$9.35   ocn920966889

Enslow Publishing
101 W. 23rd Street
Suite 240
New York, NY 10011
USA

enslow.com

Tricia Yearling

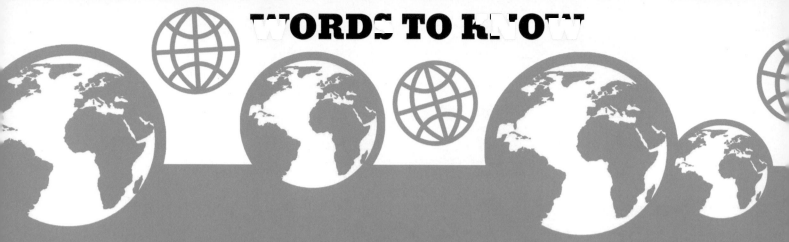

WORDS TO KNOW

browser—How you access the World Wide Web.

domain—The area that a website takes up on the World Wide Web.

hypertext markup language (HTML)—A way of writing data so it can be accessed on the World Wide Web.

hypertext transfer protocol (HTTP)—The first four letters in most web addresses; how information is easily accessed on the World Wide Web.

Internet—A system of computers linked together to share information.

Internet service provider (ISP)—a company that provides Internet service.

network—A system of data, computers, or anything else linked together.

uniform resource locator (URL)—A web address.

web page—The images and information in your browser window.

website—A set of places filled with similar information on the World Wide Web.

World Wide Web—A way for you to access the Internet.

CONTENTS

You can access all kinds of information on the World Wide Web!

What in the World Is the World Wide Web?

If you want to look up information easily and quickly, the best way is to use the World Wide Web. The World Wide Web, or the Web, can be found using the Internet on your computer. It is like having a library, movie theatre, television network, radio, and an art gallery all at once. You can discover information about anything you'd like. Learn about animals, places, people, sports, and music.

The Difference Between the Internet and the World Wide Web

Many people think that the Internet and the World Wide Web are the same thing. This is not true. The Web is part of the Internet. The Internet is the network of computers all over the world. The Web is what you access through the Internet. This includes any web page you visit or any website you look at.

The most common languages used on the World Wide Web are (in order) English, Chinese, Spanish, Japanese, and Portuguese.

An Internet service provider (ISP) installs the Internet in your home and connects it to your computer.

ISPs

To gain access to the World Wide Web, you'll need an Internet service provider (ISP). These are companies that will install the Internet in your home. They will hook your computer up to the Internet. Some of these companies include Comcast, Time Warner Cable, and Verizon. Many times you can get phone, Internet, and cable TV in the same package that you pay for. Each computer has its own ISP address. This is like a digital fingerprint that is yours and yours alone. You are the only one in the world with that particular ISP address.

A Brief History of the World Wide Web

The World Wide Web isn't that old. In fact, it's likely that when your parents and grandparents were your age, there was very little, if any, access to the World Wide Web or the Internet.

Sir Tim Berners-Lee

In 1989, a computer scientist named Sir Tim Berners-Lee created the World Wide Web. At the time, the Internet had already been invented. There was no way to truly connect

every page and user in a common way. Berners-Lee created many of the ideas that are still used today. HTML (hypertext markup language) is the basic and universal formatting, or setup, for websites. A URL (uniform resource identifier) is a unique address used to locate and identify each resource on the Web. HTTP (hypertext transfer protocol) allows for the access of linked resources from across the Web. This is why all web addresses start with http.

The Web is a new invention that parents and grandparents probably didn't have when they were young.

At first, the Web was only used by a particular group of scientists, but soon the Internet became more popular and more people had personal computers at home. It became clear that everyone needed access to the Web. So in 1991, the Web was launched for the world to use.

Early Websites

Between 1991 and 1995, many organizations, programs, and companies began creating Web addresses. Some are still in use today. Some of the earliest websites include IMDB (Internet

Tim Berners-Lee is sometimes called the Father of the World Wide Web.

Movie Database), which is a great way to look up your favorite actors, movies, and directors. Whitehouse.gov, which is the official website of the White House—home of the president of the United States—was created in 1994. Probably the most popular of the early websites still in use is the search engine Yahoo!.

Expansion of the World Wide Web

By 1996, the Web had become so widely used that it was clearly a good way to advertise. Advertisements and commercials began appearing on web pages. This lead to a boom in websites and online companies, such as Amazon.

Today, it is impossible to tell just how many web pages there are on the Web. Some pages are private and can only be accessed by their creators. But in March 2014, the 25th anniversary of the invention of the Web, there were an estimated 1.83 billion public websites.

Using the World Wide Web

One of the main benefits of the Web is that it is readily available. It can be made to work on any device, such as a smartphone, computer, or tablet. It can also work with any form of data or software and in any language. It is also decentralized, which means anyone can create a website.

Domains

When someone creates a website, he or she gets a domain. A domain is the actual address of the website. For example,

enslow.com is a domain name. So is google.com and whitehouse.gov. Some websites end in .com, which means that they are for a company. Others end in .gov, which are operated by a government agency. Sites that end in .edu are educational and usually run by schools or colleges. Originally, most Web addresses began with www. However, it is not necessary for a website to begin with www. That was just an early way to show that the website was using the Web. Today, you don't have to type in the www before a Web address.

Accessing the World Wide Web

To look at web pages, you'll need a Web browser. This may already be on your computer. Web browsers include Google Chrome, Firefox, and Safari.

Tim Berners-Lee became Sir Tim Berners-Lee in 2004. He was knighted by Queen Elizabeth II for his work on the World Wide Web.

Each of these has a specific icon, or picture, on your computer that can usually be found on your computer's desktop.

Most browsers have a box at the top of the page. This is where you type in the address, or domain name. One example of a website is enslow.com. The address or

domain is also referred to as a URL (uniform resource locator). This simply means that every website is unique and must remain that way. Could you imagine the confusion if there were several websites with the same name? It would be much harder to use the Web.

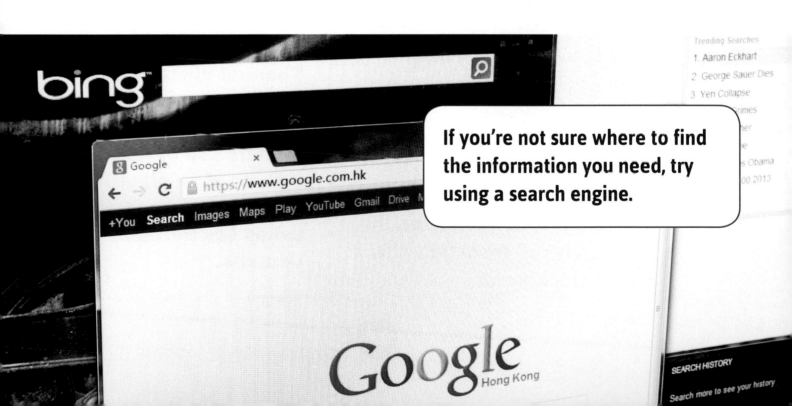

If you're not sure where to find the information you need, try using a search engine.

If you do not know the address that you're looking for, a good way to find it is to use a search engine. Examples of search engines include yahoo.com, google.com, and bing.com. In order to search, simply type in the search box what it is you are looking for. For example, you can type "pandas" if you are doing a project on pandas for school. You could also type in "latest soccer scores" if you're looking for something more specific. Remember to be as specific as possible. There are billions of web pages, and many of them may not have what you're looking for. The more details you type into your search engine, the more likely you are to find what it is you're looking for.

The first photo was uploaded to the Web in 1992. Sir Tim Berners-Lee posted a photo of an all-girl physics rock band called Les Horribles Cernetts.

Tips and Tricks for Using the World Wide Web

Hypertext is a way to write websites and domain names easily. They are easily identified because they are often in a different color or are underlined. To move around on the World Wide Web, simply use your mouse to click on the colored words. These are called hyperlinks. They will connect you to other websites.

It's easy to make your way around a website by clicking on the colored words, called hyperlinks.

Menus

Many websites have a home page that contains a menu. It tells you what is on the website. Usually, these menus have hyperlinks that will take you directly to the information you're looking for. When you click on a hyperlink in a menu, it gets more and more specific. Eventually, you will reach a page with no more hyperlinks.

Bookmarks

Sometimes you visit a website often. Instead of typing in the address every time, you can save it to your bookmarks. In most browsers, there is an option in the main menu at the top of the screen called Bookmarks. In some browsers, these are called Favorites. To save a website, simply click on the button labeled Bookmarks or Favorites. A drop-down menu will appear that will read something like, "Add website to bookmarks." Click that option. You can save the link in a toolbar on your browser's window,

Berners-Lee considered calling the World Wide Web Information Mesh, the Information Mine, and Mine of Information.

Make it easy to get back to websites you visit often by making a bookmark or favorite.

or in the Bookmarks menu. To get to the website again, you simply have to click on the link in the Bookmarks or Favorites. Then the wonderful World Wide Web will take you there!

The Web has made surfing the Internet easier. Everyone can access the information on the Internet. Anyone can have their own website. Everyone can get almost anything they need with the click of a button.

So, go! Explore the World Wide Web. Research elephants or football teams. Listen to music or watch a video. Create your own website!

But always ask an adult before going online. Ask permission before going on certain websites or buying anything on the Internet. Make sure an adult approves of your choices before you give out any personal information online.

To learn about the power of the Web, try to search for something you're interested in.

1. Open your computer's Web browser. Browsers include Google Chrome, Safari, Firefox, and Internet Explorer.

2. On the home page, there should be a search field or a bar that says something like "Search." Maybe there is a little magnifying glass icon in or near it.

3. Using your mouse, move the cursor, or the little arrow that moves when you move the mouse, to the box and click. A blinking line should appear in the search field just like in a word processor. This is your browser telling you that it is waiting for a command.

4. Type in "Carl Sagan."

5. A page should appear in your browser that shows a photo, or several, of astrophysicist Carl Sagan. Depending on which browser you're

using, you might also be able to get more information by just looking at the search results, such as a short biography, books he wrote, or his memorable quotes.

6. In Google, for example, the first website listed is the Carl Sagan Portal, or carlsagan.com.

7. Place your mouse's cursor over the Carl Sagan Portal. The text might become underlined or change colors.

8. Click on the words "the Carl Sagan Portal."

9. The welcome page of Carl Sagan's website will appear and show you all about Carl Sagan's life and work.

Harris County Public Library
Houston, Texas

LEARN MORE

Books

Gifford, Clive. *Computer Networks (Get Connected to Digital Literacy)*. New York: Crabtree Publishing, 2015.

McHugh, Jeff. *Maintaining a Positive Digital Footprint (Information Explorer Junior)*. Ann Arbor, MI: Cherry Lake Publishing, 2014

Owings, Lisa. *Stay Safe Online (Library Smarts)*. New York: Lerner Publications, 2013.

Websites

easyscienceforkids.com/all-about-computers
Computer history.

sciencekids.co.nz/sciencefacts/technology/internet.html
Facts about the Internet.

surfnetkids.com
Online resources for kids about computers and the Internet.

INDEX

Published in 2016 by Enslow Publishing, LLC.
101 W. 23rd Street, Suite 240, New York, NY 10011

Copyright © 2016 by Enslow Publishing, LLC.
All rights reserved.

No part of this book may be reproduced by any means without the written permission of the publisher.

Library of Congress Cataloging-in-Publication Data

Yearling, Tricia., author.
  The World Wide Web : what it is and how to use it / Tricia Yearling.
    pages cm. — (Zoom in on technology)
  Includes bibliographical references and index.
  ISBN 978-0-7660-7388-3 (library bound) — ISBN 978-0-7660-7386-9 (pbk.)—
  ISBN 978-0-7660-7387-6 (6-pack)
  1. World Wide Web—Juvenile literature. 2. Web sites—Juvenile literature. 3. Internet—Juvenile literature.
4. Online bibliographic searching—Juvenile literature. I. Title.
  TK5105.875.I57Y43 2016
  025.042—dc23
                                      2015034189

Printed in the United States of America

To Our Readers: We have done our best to make sure all website addresses in this book were active and appropriate when we went to press. However, the author and the publisher have no control over and assume no liability for the material available on those websites or on any websites they may link to. Any comments or suggestions can be sent by e-mail to customerservice@enslow.com.

Photo Credits: Cover, p. 1 mstanley/Shutterstock.com; gst/Shutterstock.com (globe backgrounds and headers throughout book); p. 4 iStockphoto.com/Christopher Futcher; p. 6 Sakuoka/Shutterstock.com; p. 7 Ryan McVay/Stockbyte/Thinkstock; p. 9 Fuse/Thinkstock; p. 10 Catrina Genovese/Hulton Archive/Getty Images; p. 14 LEWISWHYLD/AFP/Getty Images; p. 15 iStockphoto.com/Yongyuan Dai; p. 18 SergiyN/Shutterstock.com; p. 20 iStockphoto.com/tomeng.